TANKS

The Rourke Guides are a series of scientific and technical books. All measurements are shown in the Metric System. This is the system the scientific community uses world wide. A small conversion chart below will help those not familiar with the system.

In addition, we, the publishers have listed European terminology with American equivalents.

Metric System Conversion Chart

Unit		U.S. Equivalent	
millimetre, millimeter	(mm)	.039	inch
centimetre, centimeter	(cm)	.39	inch
metre, meter	(m)	39.4	inches
kilometre, kilometer	(km)	.62	mile
gram	(g)	15.4	grains
kilogram	(kg)	2.2	pounds
litre, liter	(l)	1.05	quarts
cubic centimetre, centimeter	(cc)	.061	cubic inch
tonne, ton	(tn)	2000	pounds

Terminology Aid

colour	— color	queued	— lined up
tonne	— ton	RPM	— revolutions per minute
defence	— defense	stabilise	— stabilize
armour	— armor	organise	— organize
aeroplane	— airplane	fulfil	— fulfill
centre	— center	customise	— customize
calibre	— caliber	£, pound	— $2.00
favour	— favor	honour	— honor
manoeuvre	— maneuver	valour	— valor
programme	— program	sledges	— sleds
BHP	— braking horse power	ploughshares —	plowshares (blade of plow)
tyre	— tire	invalided out —	medical discharge
petrol	— gasoline	labour	— labor
neighbour	— neighbor	odours	— odor
harbour	— harbor	fibres	— fibers
practise	— practice	neutralise	— neutralize
amphitheatre —	amphitheater		

TANKS

by Clive Anson
Illustrated by Ross Wardle
and Doug Post

THE ROURKE CORPORATION
Windermere, Florida

©1982 The Rourke Corporation, Inc.

Published by Granada Publishing 1981
Copyright ©Granada

Published by The Rourke Corporation, Inc., P.O. Box 711,
Windermere, Florida 32786. Copyright ©1982 by The Rourke Corporation, Inc. All copyrights reserved. No part of this book may be
reproduced in any form without written permission from the
publisher. Printed in the United States of America.

Library of Congress Cataloging in Publication Data

Anson, Clive.
  Tanks.

  (Rourke guide)
  Reprint. Originally published: London: Granada,
1981. (Granada guide)
  Includes index.
  Summary: Pictures and text trace the history of
tanks, depicting those from a number of countries.
  1. Tanks (Military science) — Juvenile literature.
[1. Tanks (Military science)]   I. Wardle, Ross, ill.
II. Post, Doug, ill.   III. Title.   IV. Series.
UG446.5.A58   1982   358'.18   82-9034
ISBN 0-86592-762-6   AACR2

Contents

Early Beginnings

Tanks are a phenomenon of the twentieth century. The cruel trench warfare of World War I spurred the development of a weapon which could bring to an end the static conflict that had taken so many lives. The first tanks were crude weapons, crudely used, and bore only a faint resemblance to today's sophisticated main battle tank (MBT). The huge technological advances of three-quarters of a century have been accompanied by an awareness of the needs of society, too, so while today's tanks use lasers and silicon chips to ensure accurate shooting, at the same time their engines must be able to run cleanly on whatever fuels are available. The environment must not suffer – at least not in peacetime.

The first tank to go to war was the British Mark IV in 1916.

Mark IV tank

Challenger

Over 60 years later, Britain's Challenger is a far cry from the Mark IV.

Early tanks were recognizable by their rhomboidal or 'lozenge' shape, and guns which could only fire on one side of the tank. Lozenge-shaped hulls were quickly replaced by more compact hulls which gave better protection, allowed the tank to be more mobile, and permitted revolving turrets. Light tanks were produced as small, fast vehicles for reconnaissance, while heavy tanks were designed to smash the massive defensive fortifications which were a feature of the early twentieth century. Medium tanks formed the backbone of armoured forces, although they were still used in support of foot soldiers and therefore rarely used above walking speed. Thirty years were to pass before it was realized that one tank could perform nearly all of these duties, and the main battle tank came into being.

Firepower, Mobility, Protection

Most battles have been won by the army which has made the best use of its soldiers' weapons, their protection and their mobility. So Boadicea's chariots were effective only until the Romans found ways of obstructing them. Knights in armour were similarly vulnerable when knocked off their horses.

The knight on his horse was a fighting unit, but without his horse the knight could not move.

A pattern began to emerge: a balance between firepower, mobility and protection. A change in any one part of the pattern caused the others to change. Leonardo da Vinci saw that the invention of guns would increase the need for protection, but that this heavier armour would be difficult to move. His 'tank' design relied on men turning cranks for its mobility and this was its weakness, for men get tired very quickly. Later came the concept of 'landships'. H G Wells wrote of 'Land Ironclads' in 1903, and as First Lord of the Admiralty, Winston Churchill gave the idea his keen support. The internal combustion engine was a promising source of power; Bessemer's newly-perfected process permitted the mass-production of armour plate, and in the development of the quick-firing gun lay a suitable weapon. These then were the ingredients from which tanks could be made.

Leonardo's wooden tank of 1482 had protection for its cannon, but there was not enough space for the men needed to propel it.

The Horse

The mounted knight in armour had sacrificed freedom of movement for protection. Lightly armed cavalry, however, could still combine the horse's agility with the sabre for shock action. Mounted troops were also excellent for reconnaissance because from horseback a cavalryman can see farther. The machine gun put an end to the cavalry's command of the battlefield, for not even the most nimble horse could escape its withering fire and, as we have seen, armour was not the answer.

The motor car was a different proposition. Several people had seen the military potential of early motor vehicles, but an Englishman named Simms was the first to use these ideas in an actual fighting vehicle in 1899.

Machine guns put an end to the use of cavalry in battle, but they were still good as scouts.

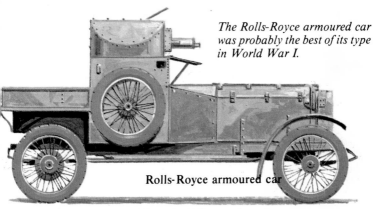

The Rolls-Royce armoured car was probably the best of its type in World War I.

Rolls-Royce armoured car

As cars increased in reliability and performance, so too did their ability to carry armour and armament. The first armoured cars consisted of standard touring cars with added armour and machine guns. The Rolls-Royce, being a particularly sturdy vehicle, was ideally suited to this conversion. Many hundreds of the Rolls-Royce armoured cars were produced and used in all the campaigns of World War I and for many years afterwards.

Tracks

A horse could carry its rider and his personal equipment across country, but for anything larger the traditional answer had always been to use the horse to pull loaded carts or sledges. The artillery and baggage trains of armies had for a long time been horse-drawn. The coming of the motor car did not immediately change this situation, and in 1914 the majority of both the German and the Allied Armies' equipment was dependent on horse power. Interest in cross-country mobility was increasing, but armoured cars were only effective on roads, so attention turned to agricultural tractors which could cope easily with rough ground. Several attempts

Holt tractor

The American Holt tractor, built in 1906, was the first practical cross-country vehicle.

had been made to imitate the walking action of animals, but only when the 'footed wheel' was logically developed into the caterpillar track was it possible to make the best use of the powerful engines then becoming available.

Killen-Strait tractor

The Killen-Strait tractor was later fitted with the body of an armoured car.

Tracked vehicles were first seen as a means of towing artillery. Early artillery tractors were converted steam traction engines from the commercial market. It was not long before far-sighted military engineers realized that in the caterpillar track lay the means of giving cross-country mobility to an armoured vehicle. At first, armoured bodies were simply mounted on caterpillar tractors, but soon afterwards a specially-designed tracked chassis was built and the tank was born.

World War I

The cavalry skirmishes and armoured car actions of the last few months of 1914 quickly gave way to a stalemate as both sides constructed massive defensive lines of trenches, and their infantry and artillery began the long process of wearing down the enemy.

The most significant weapons of war of this period were the machine gun and barbed wire. The machine gun had been used before, and the British Vickers and the German Maxim each represented the peak of the development of this weapon – perhaps best illustrated by the fact that the Vickers gun remained the British Army's standard medium machine gun for 54 years.

Barbed wire was a simple idea, originally intended to prevent the straying of cattle. When placed around trenches it would hinder and delay advancing troops long enough for the murderous machine gun fire to kill or wound many of them. Faced with such odds, it is not surprising that troops were reluctant to advance into almost certain death – although two million soldiers lost their lives this way. Military leaders grasped at anything which could bring an end to this carnage, and a machine which could crush barbed wire, cross trenches and yet withstand machine gun fire appeared to hold the answer. It was, of course, the tank.

The deep, muddy shell craters, the trenches and the barbed wire of World War I meant that neither side could win – until the tank changed it all.

The Secret Weapon

In July 1915 an English firm was given a contract to develop and build a tracked armoured vehicle, nicknamed 'Little Willie'. The vehicle was not suitable for combat, but the problem of mobility was at last solved. In the next version, 'Big Willie', the tracks ran all round the hull in a rhomboidal shape to ensure that as much track as possible remained on the ground to aid in trench crossing. A gun was fitted on each side in a 'sponson'. Big Willie was re-named 'Mother' and demonstrated to Churchill's Landships Committee in January 1916. Two weeks later 100 more were ordered and work began to raise and train a force to operate them. For secrecy this force became known as the 'Heavy Section, Machine Gun Corps' and its vehicles were described as 'Water Carriers', from which the name 'Tank' comes.

Lieutenant Colonel Swinton, the force commander, wanted to wait until his hundred tanks and their crews were fully prepared, then to use them in one decisive

'Mother' was the pattern for the Mark I, the first production tank.

Mark I 'Mother'

'Little Willie'

'Little Willie' was the first tracked armoured vehicle.

breakthrough. The Army Staff was less patient and so in September 1916 some thirty tanks, thinly spread among the infantry, attacked the German lines at Flers, on the Somme. The tanks were a success, but the element of surprise was lost and critics condemned tanks as a waste of time, effort and money. Field Marshal Haig, however, ordered a thousand more tanks, and Swinton was glad to have such support.

Mark IV tank

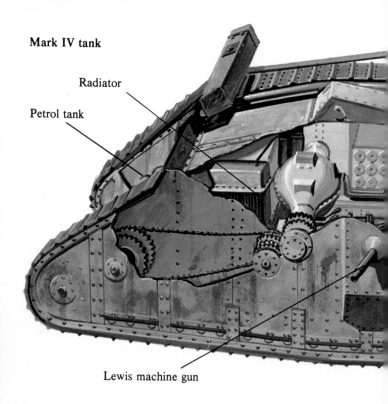

Radiator

Petrol tank

Lewis machine gun

The First Real Tank

Haig's 1,000 tanks were a great improvement on the
Mark Is which had impressed him on the Somme in
September 1916. By taking note of the lessons learnt,
the designers had come up with the Mark IV, and this
was the tank which was produced in large quantities. It
had thicker armour and a better engine installation.
Internal arrangements for the crews were also improved,
but even so, the crew had to fight in a cramped, hot,
fume-laden, dark and noisy compartment – and the
enemy was firing at them, too! The Mark IV was

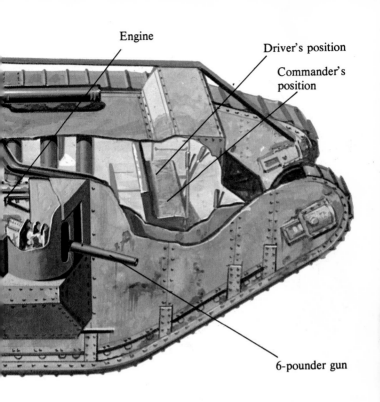

Engine

Driver's position

Commander's position

6-pounder gun

Eight men were needed to operate the Mark IV tank; Commander, Driver, 2 Gunners on each side and 2 Gearsmen at the rear. The 105 HP Daimler engine gave the 28 ton tank a top speed of just under 4 mph.

produced in two forms – some armed with two 6-pounder guns (that is, a gun firing a 6 lb shell) and known as 'males', others known as 'females' and armed with machine guns alone. Females were intended to tackle infantry to allow the males to engage enemy defences unhindered. It is of interest to note that 'Mother' was a male tank!

The First Tank Battle

The tank's baptism of fire at Flers was greeted with mixed feelings by the Allied Army Staffs. On the part of the 'Heavy Section, Machine Gun Corps', however, there was nothing but enthusiasm and the crews wanted another chance to prove themselves. Their opportunity came in November 1917 at the Battle of Cambrai. A force of 450 Mark IV tanks was assembled for an attack on the heavily fortified Hindenburg Line under cover of darkness. Without the artillery barrage which usually preceded an attack, the force of tanks had the benefit of surprise. They were able to advance up to five miles into enemy territory with devastating effects on German morale. Leading tanks tore huge gaps in the German

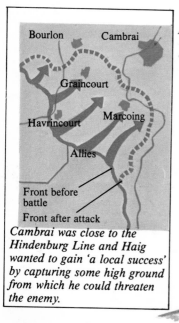

The Battle of Cambrai took place on firm ground which had not been shelled, so the tanks could advance rapidly.

Cambrai was close to the Hindenburg Line and Haig wanted to gain 'a local success' by capturing some high ground from which he could threaten the enemy.

wire and machine-gunned the trenches; following tanks crossed the trenches, using special 'fascines' – large bundles of wood; infantry then 'mopped-up' any remaining resistance in the trenches and followed the advancing tanks.

As an isolated action, the Battle of Cambrai was an outstanding success, although a lot of the captured ground was soon lost to a German counter-attack. The Tank Corps, as it was now known, had achieved more than expected and it was clear that, from now on, the tank would feature prominently on the battlefield.

The Idea Spreads

The French Army were only about six months behind the British Army in designing their own tank. They also intended their tank to crush barbed wire and cross trenches, but they viewed it more as assault artillery, overlooking the value of shock action which had been proved at Cambrai. The Schneider tank had a boat-shaped hull with a wire-cutter forming a 'prow', and was armed with a 75 mm gun on the right hand side. It was followed by the St Chamond tank, a longer, heavier tank with the same boat-shaped hull, this time with a centrally-mounted gun. These French tanks were not very successful, and it was in the production of light tanks that the French excelled.

The Germans had pressed some captured British tanks into service, and by December 1917 four tank companies had been equipped in this way. Their own development had begun in October 1916 after the appearance of the Mark I at Flers, and the result was called the A7V (after the design department of the War

France's St Chamond tank weighed 22 tons and was armed with a 75 mm gun.

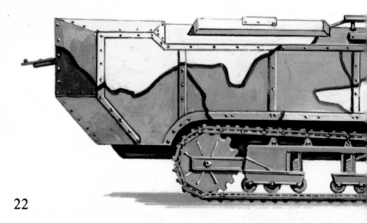

Germany's A7V had armour up to 30 mm thick but was too high.

Ministry responsible). It was a massive armoured box, armed with a Russian 57 mm gun (the same calibre as British guns). Trench crossing was a weakness of the A7V, but its suspension was far better than any other of the time and it allowed the A7V to travel at 8 mph on good ground. About twenty tanks were made before the Armistice ended the war, but the Germans had learnt the value of tanks the hard way.

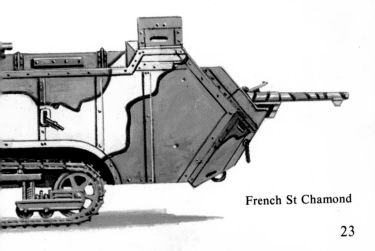

French St Chamond

Between the Wars

The horror of war had left its mark on almost every country in the world and no-one wanted to see it repeated. It had been expected by many to be a 'war to end wars', and the victorious Allies pinned their faith on disarmament. In the Treaty of Versailles the defeated German Army was forbidden to possess tanks or armoured cars. There were now pressing demands for funds which had been devoted to defence to rebuild industry and society. The United States took the view that the rest of the world could attend to itself. In Britain

it was assumed that there would be no war for at least ten years. In these circumstances there were no funds for tank forces, and most armies reverted to their pre-1914 state, relying on infantry, artillery and horse-drawn transport. In Russia the Revolution meant that progress toward mechanization was slow, and Britain and France held the lead in tank design.

If the desire for peace and the unwillingness to spend money on armaments meant that European armies were in decline, there was no slowing down the minds which had foreseen the use of tanks. Officers who had commanded tank units developed concepts of mech-anized armies which would be based on tanks rather than infantry.

Swords into ploughshares – as the threat of war passed, tanks were scrapped in large numbers.

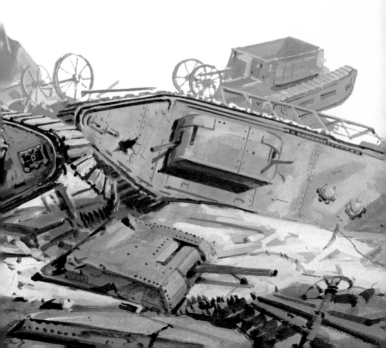

Tank Pioneers

At the time of Cambrai, Lieutenant Colonel J F C Fuller was an officer on the Staff of the Tank Corps, responsible for the planning of tank operations until the defeat of Germany. After the war he continued to write articles and essays stressing his views that the tank had brought a new age of mobility to the battlefield, and that it could not be abandoned as quickly as it had been adopted. He argued for the formation of an experimental armoured brigade, but as always this was hampered by lack of money.

Another name to emerge at the same time was that of Captain Basil Liddell Hart. Wounded in the war, he had been invalided out of the Army and became a journalist, joining in the debate on the future composition of the British Army. He saw the value of tanks in their shock action – in being able to attack from an unexpected direction.

Basil Liddell Hart

Basil Liddell Hart saw tanks as a way of preventing the enormous casualties of trench warfare by restoring movement to the battlefield. His views were ignored in Britain.

26

J F C Fuller

Fuller tried to convince the authorities that the tank should be the dominant weapon in battle. He failed, but in Germany Guderian succeeded.

In Germany, too, serious thought was given to the use of tanks. Denied any form of offensive weapon, the German Army began to train secretly with dummy tanks built on ordinary cars. The most prominent German theorist of the 1930s was Captain Heinz Guderian. Like Fuller and Liddell Hart, Guderian realized that rather than keeping tanks at infantry speed, infantry and artillery would have to be given the same mobility as tanks. This became the German 'Blitzkrieg' concept – that of 'lightning war'.

The single thread running through all these theories was the realization that the tank is not a defensive weapon. It is often said that attack is the best form of defence, and this argument began to make sense as the world anxiously viewed Hitler's re-arming of Germany in the 1930s. When the Spanish Civil War began in 1936, Guderian's theories were put to the test by German troops fighting on General Franco's side.

Tanks of the 30s

Most of the advances in tank design between the wars came from private firms rather than military designers. Vickers produced many tanks in Britain. Their 6 ton tank was bought by twelve countries, while their light tanks were sold around the world. French industry was also active, with the firms of Renault and Hotchkiss playing major parts. The Renault R-35 tank was sold to several countries. The S-35 was produced by SOMUA and was the best-designed French tank of the 1930s. Though Germany was forbidden to possess tanks, by 1930 the two famous firms of Krupp and Rheinmetall were designing and building tanks. Testing was carried out secretly in Russia. The United States lagged behind in its tank forces after a decision that tanks should be controlled by the Infantry. Officials were therefore unenthusiastic about J W Christie's revolutionary suspension design, which gave a tremendous increase in cross-country capability and road speed. Christie's ideas were adopted in Britain and Russia, but not in his own country.

American Christie T3

The S-35 was made from well-sloped cast armour sections. Its top speed was 25 mph.

The American T3 used Christie's suspension and had a speed of 47 mph when the tracks were removed. Only a few were made.

29

World War II

The warning signals of the Spanish Civil War were ignored, so when Germany attacked France and Poland in 1939 the lessons of Blitzkrieg were learnt. Her troops pushed quickly round the edges of the French Maginot Line in their well-proven tanks. The light PzKpfw I and II (Panzer Kampfwagen – armoured fighting vehicle) and the medium PzKpfw III and IV tanks were designed to fight as a team in a Panzer Division, while against them was an assortment of French tanks. The British Expeditionary Force in France was equipped with light tanks (the Mark VI, armed with a machine gun) and infantry tanks (the Mark I and II, known as 'Matildas'). Infantry tanks were slow, being designed to keep pace

Panzers in France 1940

with foot soldiers, but were better armed and much more heavily armoured than light tanks.

German tanks were generally faster and better armed than their opponents and the only virtue of the Matilda was its comparative immunity to German tank guns. It may have been a blessing in disguise when all the BEF's tanks were abandoned in the 1940 evacuation from Dunkirk.

The story had been much the same in Poland. The Polish Army had been attracted by the idea of 'tankettes' (small 1- or 2-man machine gun carriers) in the 1920s and had equipped many of its units with them, so that when the need came it could not afford proper tanks. Even so the Poles put up a stiff resistance but could not hold out for long against the relentless advance of ten divisions of armour.

By-passing French defences allowed Panzer divisions to advance rapidly to the English Channel. In the air, bombers were used to harass the retreating army.

The Race is On

The next tank encounters took place in the Western Desert of North Africa and on the steppes of Russia in 1941. In the desert, British Matildas and Crusaders fought German PzKpfw IIIs, IVs and Italian M11/39s and, while German tank guns were still superior, in other respects British and German tanks were evenly matched. The Italians were in the same position as the BEF in France in 1939: undergunned and under-armoured.

The German 88 mm anti-aircraft gun had been found to be very effective against tanks in the Spanish Civil War and it was used to great effect in the desert, inflicting heavy losses on the fast but thin-skinned British Crusaders. Nevertheless, the Italians were sufficiently impressed by the speed of the Crusader to make their own copy.

Hitler's invasion of Russia brought the Panzer Divisions into contact with Soviet armour. Here, fast BT-7 tanks showed the value of high speed, while the heavy KV-1 tanks were almost immune to anti-tank fire.

Both Germany and the Allies put their maximum effort into developing better tanks during this time, but quality was of no use without quantity. When the United States entered the war in December 1941 the enormous production facilities of the American motor industry were turned to tank production and entire new factories – tank arsenals – were built. As the United States was safe from bombing attacks, production was unhindered, and this fact alone was an enormous contribution to the eventual Allied victory.

Tank production was one of the keys to victory. Factories in Britain and Germany were disrupted by bombing but in the United States production ran at full speed night and day. Here, post-war M48s are being mass-produced in Detroit in 1952.

British and German Tanks

As we saw earlier, the main features of all tanks fall into three categories: mobility, firepower and protection. The importance given to each aspect at the expense of the others governs the fighting qualities of the tank.

In mobility, the doctrine of Blitzkrieg dictated that German tanks should be powerful and fast, while British tanks were built for more leisurely progress. German tanks used torsion bar suspension, a recent development which could be incorporated in the hull floor. British infantry tanks had generally less sophisticated suspensions bolted on to the hull sides. The Crusader broke away from this with its Christie suspension which, together with its 340 horsepower Liberty engine, gave it a top speed of 27 mph.

For a variety of reasons, German tank guns were more powerful than those of the Allies throughout nearly all the war. In many cases, excellent guns designed in Britain or the United States were refused by military authorities who could see no need for improvements, but by the end of 1945 better guns were coming into use.

Protection, the defensive side of tank design, was the strongest feature of British tanks. The Matilda and Churchill could both withstand most German weapons. Later, the Panther redressed the balance with its well sloped armour.

The tanks shown on the facing page are not necessarily equals, but are shown to illustrate the wide variety of features. The production figures have been included to give an idea of the scale on which tanks were produced. Overall, Britain produced 24,803 tanks while Germany produced 24,360. To Britain's figure, however, the American figure of 88,410 must be added, and one reason for Allied victory is now clear.

Matilda II (2987 produced). Two diesel engines gave a speed of 15 mph. Armour: 78 mm Gun: 2 pounder (40 mm).

PzKpfwIII series (5644 produced). 230 hp petrol engine gave a speed of 20 mph. Armour: up to 18 mm. Gun: 37 mm to 50 mm.

Crusader Mark II (5300 produced). 340 hp engine gave speed of 27 mph. Armour: 49 mm. Gun: 6 pounder (57 mm).

PzKpfw IVE (9000 produced). 300 hp petrol engine gave a speed of 21 mph. Armour: up to 30 mm. Gun: 75 mm.

Churchill Mark III (5640 produced). 350 hp petrol engine gave a speed of 15 mph. Armour: 102 mm. Gun: 6 pounder.

PzKpfw V Panther (5976 produced). 650 hp petrol engine gave a speed of 28.5 mph. Armour: up to 110 mm. Gun: 75 mm High Velocity.

Anti-Tank Weapons

When tanks had armour that was little more than a centimetre thick, it was possible for even a well-aimed rifle shot to cause some damage. Anti-tank rifles (long, heavy weapons which fired armour-piercing bullets at a very high velocity, yet could still be carried by one man) were in widespread use. But they were far from popular with the soldiers who had to carry and fire them. Larger anti-tank guns were mounted on wheels and towed by trucks or even horses.

A novel principle, the so-called 'hollow charge', can, when used to focus the force of an explosive, penetrate several times its own diameter into steel or concrete. Using the hollow charge principle would therefore allow a 5 cm shell to penetrate up to 15 cm of armour, and the shell was found to be more effective if fired at a fairly low

The M6A2 heavy anti-tank mine

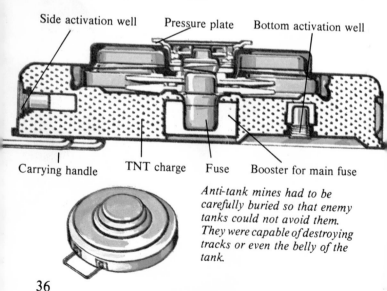

Side activation well   Pressure plate   Bottom activation well

Carrying handle   TNT charge   Fuse   Booster for main fuse

Anti-tank mines had to be carefully buried so that enemy tanks could not avoid them. They were capable of destroying tracks or even the belly of the tank.

Bazooka rocker launcher

'Bazooka' was a nickname given to the American rocket launcher. It had a range of about 200 metres and would penetrate up to 12 cm of armour.

velocity, such as that of a rocket. Thus the 'Bazooka' was born, although hollow charges could also be fired from artillery and tank guns. About a quarter of all tank losses were due to hollow charge weapons.

Mines were another effective way of destroying tanks but, because a mine cannot tell the difference between friend and foe, they became a two-edged weapon. Specially-modified tanks were used to clear minefields, but even so, about one in six of all tanks lost was destroyed by mines.

While it was useful for infantry to have their own anti-tank weapons, one fact was becoming clear. The only way to defeat a tank formation is with more tanks, for their mobility enables them to outflank static antitank guns and minefields.

37

The Allies Strike Back

The Lend-Lease Act passed in America in March of 1941 had made M3 Grant and Lee medium tanks available to the British Army, to make up for the heavy losses of the first two years of fighting. When the Japanese bombing of Pearl Harbor brought the United States into the war, their army needed tanks, too. Fortunately, production of the M4 Sherman tank was underway and these were very generously shared with the British Army – and the Russian Army also received some. There was nothing exceptional about the Sherman as a combat vehicle, but it was manufactured in such numbers that it was a war-winning tank. Nearly 50,000 were made, and many are still in use today.

M4 Sherman

The Allied invasion of Sicily in 1943 was the beginning of the attack on Hitler's Europe, and in Russia the greatest tank battle of all time took place at Kursk in July 1943. Although mainly a battle of tanks versus tanks, it was acutally the anti-tank guns of each side which inflicted the most losses. The famous Russian T-34 tank, which inspired the German Panther, made its first impact at Kursk. From Italy and from Russia, the net was closing in on Germany from both sides.

Specially-built landing craft delivered tanks and troops to the beaches of Sicily.

Landing craft

DD amphibious tank

The Battle for Europe

British, Commonwealth and American forces slowly advanced through Italy in 1943 and early 1944, but the Russians were insisting on a 'Second Front' in Europe which would force the Germans to divert troops from the Eastern Front. This chance came on 6 June, 1944, when the greatest fleet ever assembled carried Allied armies across the English Channel in 3,000 landing craft and ships. Overhead the Allied Air Forces were supreme, while few German warships dared to venture out into the Channel.

Sherman equipped for wading

Churchill bridge layer

'D-day', 6 June 1944. Amphibious tanks, bulldozers, mine-clearing tanks, bridge-layers and many other types all helped to storm the beaches.

Over 6,000 Allied tanks were landed on the beaches of Normandy and these included many strange new tanks seen for the first time. These 'funnies' included mine-clearing tanks, which beat or ploughed mines out of the path of the gun tanks which followed behind; there were bridge-laying tanks to span bridges which the retreating Germans had demolished; recovery vehicles which were tanks modified to tow damaged tanks back for repair, and self-propelled guns which gave to artillery some of the mobility of tanks. The German defenders fought hard but they were surrounded and out-numbered and their tanks were in the wrong places. They were unable to thrust the invading armies back into the sea. Soon the Allies were on their way to Germany.

Heavy Tanks

The struggle amongst tank designers to produce better tanks had an inevitable result: tanks became bigger and heavier. To fit a bigger gun to a tank, it must be wider; this makes it heavier, so it needs a bigger engine. Only the fact that tanks still had to be carried for long distances by train, and had to cross road bridges, kept the weight of tanks to reasonable limits. Britain resisted the temptation to build a heavy tank, but Germany produced the Tiger tank (Pzkpfw VI) and used it to tremendous effect in the desert, on the Russian Front, and in Normandy. The Russians developed their JS-2 Stalin tanks, and these powerful monsters led the Russian dash to Berlin. The Americans were late on the scene with a heavy tank, but their M26 Pershing was a good design and proved

The Tiger tank, with its 88 mm gun and 100 mm armour, was the scourge of Allied tanks. One tank destroyed a total of 119 Russian tanks.

Russian JS-2

The 122 mm gun of the JS-2 made a useful artillery weapon in the assault on Berlin.

to be the most enduring; its descendants are still widely used today. Tanks of this size would now be considered as main battle tanks, and in fact the Pershing was re-classified as a medium tank just after the war.

German Tiger tank

The Pacific War

When Germany surrendered on 7 May, 1945 the Allies turned their attention to the war in the Pacific. Here the Japanese Army was conducting a fanatical defence of each of the thousands of jungle-covered islands around the Pacific Ocean. The brunt of the fighting had fallen on the Americans, although British Commonwealth troops had also seen their share of combat. Tanks were not really suited to jungle warfare, but Stuart light tanks and Grant and Sherman medium tanks had been used to good effect against Japanese troops in open country and on occasions against rather out-dated enemy tanks.

When it came to liberating all the islands another approach was called for. Amphibious tanks, called 'Alligators' or LVTs were used both for fire support and also as troop carriers. The first LVT (standing for 'landing vehicle, tracked') was an unarmoured amphibious carrier known as the 'Buffalo'. When armed with machine guns, rockets or flame throwers they were ideal for the Pacific War and thousands were built. Plans for heavy tanks and guns to smash the heavy fortifications expected on the Japanese mainland were shelved when, in the first weeks of August 1945, two atomic bombs were dropped on Japan and six long years of war were brought to an end.

The coral reefs of the Pacific Islands made assault from the sea almost impossible without the use of LVTs and amphibious vehicles.

DUKW amphibious truck

LVT   Alligator

The Atomic Age

Overnight the atom bomb had rendered conventional defence worthless, and just as it seemed that the battleship was doomed to extinction, so many experts also predicted that the tank's days were over. Two things proved them wrong. First, as the Korean War showed, there would still be wars where nuclear weapons would not be used and where tanks would be indispensable. Second, when it comes to fighting on a nuclear battlefield, the tank offers a good degree of protection. In trials carried out in the Nevada desert, tanks and other military equipment were exposed to the full force of atomic bombs. Tanks were found to survive quite well – in one case a tank's engine was still running while there was no trace of a jeep which had been parked beside it. The tank's crew would perish so close to the blast, but farther away their chances of survival would be better than those of troops without any protection.

The atomic bombs dropped on Japan brought surrender and the end of the war. Tank crews are quite well protected against radiation.

Years of ''Peace''

Although World War II ended in 1945, fighting continued in several places. In the Middle East the new state of Israel struggled hard for its survival, assembling an assortment of tanks from many sources. The Korean War lasted for three years and American Shermans and Pershings showed their worth against the Soviet T-34s of the North Koreans and Chinese. British Centurions of the 8th Hussars received their baptism of fire in this war. In a succession of other wars tanks have featured too: at

Sherman

Suez in 1956; in the Indo-Pakistan Wars; in the 'Six Day War' of 1967, when brilliantly-led Israeli armour shattered the Soviet tanks of the Arab armies, and in Vietnam. The jungles of Southeast Asia might seem a strange place for American armour, but the M48 Pattons were superb at 'jungle-busting' – clearing routes through thick undergrowth, and destroying enemy bunkers. In the Middle East War of 1973, Egyptian anti-tank missiles took a heavy toll of Israel's veteran Shermans, Centurions and Pattons, but in the end the tanks won the day. Even today there are Soviet tanks in action in Afghanistan.

The Israeli army has made extensive modifications to its Shermans (left) and M48s (right)

M48

Centurion tank

British Tanks

Although Britain is no longer an imperial power, British
tank design has remained a leading influence throughout
the world. Experience in World War II had convinced
the British Army of the value of firepower and protection.
The Centurion, which first appeared in 1945, reflected
this view. It proved to be an excellent design and in its
long service with the British Army was twice fitted with
more powerful guns and up-armoured several times. It is
still in service with many armies and will continue to be
an excellent main battle tank for years to come. Its
successor, the Chieftain, shows the same emphasis on

The Centurion was the most successful tank in the world during the 1950s and 1960s.

firepower and protection – its critics say at the expense of mobility. Its 120 mm gun is the best tank gun in the world, while its armour will continue to be a tough problem for enemy tanks. It is also equipped with air filtration to enable the crew to operate the tank in contaminated surroundings, such as the nuclear battle-field. The gunner uses a sophisticated laser fire-control system and both he and the tank commander have night vision devices, enabling them to engage enemy tanks in darkness. To keep the height of the tank to a minimum, the driver's seat is in a semi-reclining position.

American Tanks

The Pershing tank, which began to enter service at the end of World War II, was the beginning of a series of American tanks which formed a logical sequence in development. The Pershing was officially called the M26 and had a 90 mm gun. During the Korean War an improved version with a new engine was introduced, and this was called the M46. It was, however, more popularly known as the 'Patton' after the famous general.

Later, a new turret was added, making the tank the M47,

The M48 is a very adaptable tank and has been modified many times. It will probably still be in service in the year 2000.

or 'Patton II', and in 1954 the M48, or 'Patton III' appeared. The M48 had many of the features of the M26, but most of it was new. The gun was still 90 mm, though, and the M48's engine was still a petrol engine. There were several models of the M48 – for instance, the model used in Vietnam was the M48A3, with a diesel engine. Diesel fuel is much less inflammable than petrol, so it is preferred to petrol in modern tanks. Then in 1959 came the M60, still similar to the M26 in appearance, but with a British 105 mm gun which was acknowledged to be among the best in the world.

M48 tank

Russian Tanks

As with both British and American tanks, Russian tank developments form a sequence which has evolved over the years. Today's T-64 and T-72 have their origins in the T-34, of which over 45,000 were made. Russia has maintained a huge industrial base since the war, producing enough tanks for her own vast army and also for those of her allies. The next model after the T-34 was the T-44, but this was only produced in small numbers. In 1949 came the first of what was to become the standard Russian tank for over ten years – the T-54. This tank, which has taken part in almost every conflict since 1950, was made in large numbers like the T-34. Simple production techniques were used, for an army as big as

Russian T-62

Many thousands of T-62s have been made and it is used by many armies throughout the world. Its turret is very cramped.

the Red Army preferred quantity to quality. So that their tanks could have a low silhouette, only soldiers up to about 1.6 metres tall are selected as tank crews. Not that tank crews are considered inferior at all – the Soviet Union is probably the only country where they have their own day. Soviet Tankmen's Day has been celebrated on 8 September every year since 1946. The T-54 was a contemporary, if not an equal, of the Centurion and M48, but it was replaced before the other two. In 1961 the T-62 made its first appearance. The main difference lay in the use of a new 115 mm smoothbore gun, whose 'arrow shot' could pierce the armour of almost every other tank.

Tanks of Other Nations

Tank manufacture is an expensive business, and few countries can afford it alone, but it is not the exclusive preserve of the military powers. When the West German Army was re-armed, one of its first decisions was that a new tank was needed to replace the American M47s then in use. Together with France and Italy the Germans embarked on a new project but France was unhappy about the design, while Italy viewed the cost with alarm.

French AMX-30

The French AMX-30 has a 105 mm gun and is fast but lightly armoured.

The S-Tank with its 105 mm gun was designed specifically for the defence of Sweden.

Swedish S-Tank

German Leopard tank

In the Leopard a very good balance between firepower, mobility and protection has been achieved. Several thousand have been made.

Germany pressed ahead with what became the Leopard; France developed the AMX-30 to suit her own priorities, and in the end Italy bought the Leopard from Germany.

Many other countries also bought the Leopard – so many that it is often called the NATO tank. France also sold its AMX-30 abroad. Sweden's neutrality called for a different type of tank, and when it appeared the S-Tank was a revolutionary design. It was turretless, the gun being aimed by moving the whole tank up and down and from side to side. While this prevents the tank from firing while on the move, it does allow an extremely low silhouette and the use of an automatic loader, making the S-Tank very useful in defence.

Those countries who can neither build their own tanks nor afford to buy new tanks often devote their resources to improving the tanks they already have. In Israel, Centurions, Shermans, Pattons and even captured Egyptian T-54s have been thoroughly modified to suit the needs of the Israeli Defence Forces – although the new heavily armoured Merkava was designed and built entirely in Israel.

Specialized Tanks

The first special-purpose armoured vehicles began to appear quite soon after the tank had made its debut in France. Old or damaged tanks were stripped of their guns and used to transport cargo or troops. Some were also used to tow damaged tanks. The American tank pioneer Christie's first designs were for self-propelled guns on tracked chassis, and France and Britain both modified tanks to carry bridges in the 1930s. Today's specialized armoured vehicles perform the same roles as their forebears, but most of these types have been

French AMX-30D
recovery vehicle

French AMX-30
bridgelayer with
folding bridge

designed for their task from the outset, using as many components of standard tanks as possible. Armoured personnel carriers are used to transport infantry on the battlefield, protecting them from enemy small arms and shell splinters. Self-propelled guns provide mobility for large artillery weapons and cover for their crews. Other tasks have to be performed in combat: there are gaps to be spanned; damaged tanks must be recovered for repair; anti-aircraft tanks are needed for air defence. For these and many other reasons there will always be a variety of specialized tanks.

Dutch YP-408
armoured personnel carrier

French 155 mm F3
self-propelled gun

Helicopters are fast and agile. With powerful missiles they can attack tanks at long range.

Scout Helicopter

German Leopard 2

The Leopard and the M1 will form the backbone of NATO into the twenty-first century.

American M1

The Future

In the wars in the Middle East it seemed to many that the anti-tank guided missile spelt the end of the tank, but still the tank goes on. New types of armour defeat the missile; new guns defeat the thicker armour, and the contest continues. One popular idea is to replace large, costly battle tanks with smaller, cheaper light tanks. Another school of thought believes that the mobility of the hovercraft and the helicopter may take the place of the protection of the armour of today's tanks. Hovercraft

Small hovercraft can carry missiles. Hovercraft such as this BN-7 can carry light tanks.

BN-7 Hovercraft

Russian T-62

The T62 is being replaced by the T72 and the T80 is now entering service.

The Chieftain is to be replaced by the Challenger in the mid 1980s.

British Challenger

were widely used in the Vietnam War, and both the American and Soviet Armies are now equipped with anti-tank helicopters, firing powerful missiles at long ranges. Shock action on the battlefield will still require a combination of the same three factors: firepower, mobility and protection, and tanks will continue to fulfil this role around the world for at least another fifty years. The twentieth century weapon will have become a weapon of the twenty-first century.

Index